NORTHWOODS COOKING COLLECTION

Pie Iron Recipes

Compiled and Edited by:
Darren Kirby

Copyright © 2015 Darren Kirby

First Printing: May, 2015

All rights reserved.

ISBN: 1508903832
ISBN-13: 9781508903833

Top cover image copyright Stephane Mignon, 8/14/2010
https://www.flickr.com/photos/topsteph53/

Middle cover image copyright Brett Neilson, 10/5/2013
https://www.flickr.com/photos/brettneilson/

Bottom cover image copyright Nicholas Tonelli, 9/2/2012
https://www.flickr.com/photos/nicholas_t/

All images used under the Creative Commons License
Images modified by Darren Kirby

OTHER WRITINGS BY DARREN KIRBY

~Nonfiction~

Pie Iron Recipes

~Novels~

Coordinates For Murder

~Short Story Collections~

Sometimes They Scream

~Short Stories~

Pins and Dolls
The Ritual
f r e q u e n c y
Two Inches of Revenge
A Push Too Far

TABLE OF CONTENTS

Introduction	1
Notes About Recipes	3

Breakfast Recipes:

French Toast With Bacon	7
Pie Iron Biscuits With Sausage Gravy	8
Bacon And Eggs Breakfast Sandwich	9
Pancakes Stuffed With Sausage	10
Pie Iron Stuffed Hashbrowns	11
Sausage And Egg Breakfast Sandwich	12
Mixed Berry Breakfast	13
Corn Bread Breakfast	14
Hashbrowns	15
Grog Cakes	16
Cheesy Tots	17
Pie Iron Cinnamon Sticks	18
Simple Cinnamon Roll Toast	19
Potato, Bacon & Egg Breakfast	20
Egg In The Nest	21
Packed Pancake Breakfast	22

Lunch/Dinner Recipes:

Tuna Melts	25
Salmon Jaffe	26
Salmon or Tuna Cristo	27
Crab Pie	28
Chicken BBQ Pie	29
Chicken Quesedillas	30
Grilled Turkey	31
Chicken Parmesan	32
Chicken Cordon Bleu	33
Greek Pie	34
Samosa Pie	35
Grilled Ham and Cheese	36
BLT Special	37
Cuban Sandwich	38
Reuben Sandwich	39
Grilled Roast Beef Sandwich	40
Burrito	41
Philly Cheesesteak	42
Bacon Cheeseburger	43
Beef Stew Pie	44
Pasties	45
Sloppy Joes	46
Meatloaf Sandwich	47
Grilled Cheese	48
Calzone	49

PB & J	50
Mac & Cheese Pocket	51
Pepper Poppers	52
Basic Pizza Pockets	53
Chicken Pot Pie	54
Spaghetti Sandwiches	55
Bologna & Cheese Sandwiches	56
Ravioli With Garlic Toast	57
Bacon & Peanut Butter	58
Baked Beans Sandwich	59
Chicken & Pineapple	60
Hot BBQ Beef Sandwich	61
Vegetarian Quesadilla	62
Easy Vegan Hobo Pie	63

Dessert Recipes:

Chocolate Caramel Pie	67
Cinnamon Bun Pie	68
Basic Fruit Turnover	69
Apple Strudel	70
Cherry Cheesecake Dessert	71
Lemon Meringue Pie	72
Peanut Butter Cup Melt	73
Sunny Peach Sandwich	74
Banana Cream Pie	75

Fluffernutter Pie	76
Cinnamon & Sugar Pie	77
Peanut Butter & Marshmallows	78
Cream Cheese & Fresh Berries	79
Nutty-Creamy-Fruity Goodness	80
Chocolate Caramel Nut Pies	81
Banana & Nutella	82
Apple & Brown Sugar	83
Peanut Butter & Apples	84
Pumpkin Pie	85
Cinnamon Balls	86
Berries & Chocolate	87
Caramel Apple Pie	88
Pineapple Delight	89
Chocolate Cheesecake	90
Campfire Chocolate Monkey Bread	91
Chocolate Overload	92

Additional Food Recipes:

Fried Potatoes	95
Grilled Mushrooms	96
Grilled Onions	97
Biscuits	98
Cornbread	99
Brie in Pastry	100

Garlic Cheese Balls	101
Grilled Steak	102
Portabella Melts	103
Honey Glazed Carrots	104
Pudgie Fried Rice	105
Helpful Hints When Using Your Pie Iron	107
Aluminum vs Cast Iron	109
Pie Iron Carry Case	111
Seasoning Your Cast Iron Pie Iron	113
About The Author	115
Connect With The Author	117

INTRODUCTION

My wife and I love to go camping. One of our most favorite things to do for food is to use our pudgie pie irons. They are versatile and so easy that kids have as much fun at meal time as adults. And while you may know that they turn out great homemade "hot pockets", they can be used for a lot more. It's possible to use just these pie irons to cook everything over a weekend camping trip, which would save a lot of weight and space when packing.

If you've never tried using a pie iron, a pudgie pie maker, a jaffel iron, or whatever name you choose to call it, you're missing out on a positively wonderful meal time treat. You'll find recipes for every meal of the day, especially desserts! And while these recipes are a good start, there's really no end to the combinations that you can come up with.

This recipe book is unique in its approach for a variety of reasons. First, you will notice that there are no bright, vibrant pictures of the food presented beautifully on colored plates in perfectly setup dining rooms and kitchens. There are a few reasons for this, including cost; getting those pictures shot is a costly endeavor. Also, it would nearly double the size of this book, meaning it would cost you more to purchase this book, and I want this to be an affordable option for everyone; camping itself is inherently cost-effective related to other vacation types, and this book needed to reflect this economy.

Another item that makes this recipe book unique is that we are solely focused on just the round/square style of pie iron. There are a variety of other pie iron designs and shapes, but they are more niche-focused and consequently have limited applications, unlike the traditional round/square pie iron. Along with staying focused on this traditional design, we have also included more recipes for these style pie irons than any other recipe book out there.

Last, not only do we cover the important stuff (food!), but we also cover a variety of related areas to consider with pie irons, such as the pros and cons of aluminum versus cast iron and best practices when using your pie irons.

So, let's dig out those pie irons and dig into some tasty food!

NOTES ABOUT THE RECIPES

You will notice that in all of these recipes, we use the generic names for the food items. That's because everyone has different tastes, and just because I like brand X, you might think it tastes nasty and you prefer brand Y. Well, use brand Y then! Experiment, try new things, make new combinations, and just have fun.

Also, a word about the bread. For these recipes, when I use the word "bread", unless you read something different, I'm just talking about your plain old white bread. Many of these recipes would be delicious and have a very different taste just by changing the bread you use. Give a marble rye a shot, or perhaps a pumpernickel. Don't just experiment with the insides of the pies, but the outsides as well.

For those who are vegetarians or just want to use less meat, substitutions are encouraged. Just like you would do for recipes you would make at home, use your favorite substitutions for the chicken, pepperoni, hamburger, and other meats that you find listed in these recipes. While fewer in number, I have included some meatless recipes as well.

In the end, these recipes are just guidelines, and you can follow them as closely or as loosely as you want. Food is meant to be enjoyed, and cooking that food should be equally enjoyable.

BREAKFAST RECIPES

FRENCH TOAST WITH BACON

Ingredients:
Bacon
Bread
Egg and milk, beaten together
Cinnamon
Butter

Directions:
1- Cook the bacon in your open pie iron. Each side holds 1-2 pieces
2- Soak 2 slices of bread in the egg and milk mixture; sprinkle each with a little bit of cinnamon
3- In each half of the pie iron put a small dab of butter, then lay in a piece of the battered bread
4- Put the bacon on one of the bread slices, and then close up the pie iron
5- Cook over the fire until golden brown

Alternatives:
* Add cheese with the bacon
* Substitute your favorite jam/jelly for the filling

PIE IRON BISCUITS WITH SAUSAGE GRAVY

Ingredients:
1/2 tray Johnsonville Original Breakfast Sausage Patties, broken into pieces
1 tbsp. all-purpose flour
1 cup 1% milk
1/4 tsp. pepper
Pinch of salt
1 can refrigerated Pillsbury Country Style Biscuits
Butter

Directions:
1- Heat skillet and cook sausage, breaking up with spoon, until browned, about 5 minutes
2- Mix in flour
3- Stir in milk, scraping up browned bits from pan, until mixture is thickened, about 2 to 3 minutes
4- Season with pepper and salt; remove from heat and set aside
5- On waxed paper on plate or back of saucepan, flatten each biscuit into a 4-inch circle
6- In each half of the pie iron put a small dab of butter, then lay in a circle of biscuit
7- Scoop 3 tbsp of sausage gravy into middle of one of the biscuit circles
8- Cover with 1 circle and close up pie iron
9- Cook over the fire until golden brown

BACON AND EGGS BREAKFAST SANDWICH

Ingredients:
Bread
Bacon
Eggs
Cheddar or Monterey Jack cheese slices

Directions:
1- Heat your pie iron slightly in the fire; don't get it too hot, or else the bacon will burn
2- Lay three strips of bacon in one half of the pie iron so that half of the bacon is in the pie iron and the other half is laying out
3- Put a piece of bread over the bacon and squish it down a bit (no air pockets)
4- Crack an egg right in the middle of your bread
5- Place a slice or two of cheese over the egg
6- Top with a second piece of bread, but don't squish it down
7- Wrap the loose ends of your bacon around the outside of the other slice of bread and close up the pie iron
8- Cook in the fire for about five to seven minutes, or until the bacon has gone crispy on the outside

Darren Kirby

PANCAKES STUFFED WITH SAUSAGE

Ingredients:
Pancake mix, prepared
Sausage links

Directions:
1- Pour prepared pancake mix into one half of the pie iron
2- Add 2-3 sausage links into the pancake mix
3- Add a little more pancake mix, then close up the pie iron
4- Cook over the fire until golden brown

PIE IRON STUFFED HASHBROWNS

Ingredients:
1 pound of hashbrowns, frozen
8 oz. sour cream
1/2 cup shredded cheddar cheese
1 green onion, thinly sliced
4 slices of bacon, cooked and crumbled
Butter

Directions:
1- Put a dab of butter in one half of the pie iron, then add a thin layer of hash browns to pie iron
2- In a separate bowl mix together sour cream, green onion and bacon
3- Add approximately 2 tablespoons of sour cream mixture on top of hash browns, spreading out to the edges
4- Sprinkle cheese over sour cream mixture followed with another layer of hash browns
5- Add a dab of butter on top of hash browns, then close up the pie iron and then cook approximately 3 minutes per sides

SAUSAGE AND EGG BREAKFAST SANDWICH

Ingredients:
Bread
Eggs
Sausage links
Cheddar cheese slices
Butter

Directions:
1- Beat eggs in small bowl
2- Put a dab of butter in one half of the pie iron, then add a slice of bread pressing it down
3- Pour eggs into the divot in the bread
4- Add a slice of cheese over the eggs, then add sausage over the cheese
5- Add second slice of bread, and put a dab of butter on this slice
6- Close up the pie iron and then cook the egg is set and cheese is melted, turning frequently

MIXED BERRY BREAKFAST

Ingredients:
Bread
Cream cheese
Frozen mixed berries
White chocolate, chopped
Confectioners sugar, to serve
Maple syrup, to serve
Butter

Directions:
1- Put a dab of butter in one half of the pie iron and add a slice of bread
2- Spread cream cheese on bread slice, then add berries
3- Sprinkle chopped white chocolate over berries
4- Add another slice of bread, then add a bad of butter on the bread
5- Close up the pie iron and cook until golden brown
6- Dust with confectioner sugar and serve with maple syrup

CORN BREAD BREAKFAST

Ingredients:
1 box corn bread mix
Pre-cooked bacon strips
Grated cheese (any kind)
Chopped onion
Butter

Directions:
1- Prepare corn bread mix according to directions
2- Add bacon, cheese and onions to corn bread mixture
3- Grease pie iron with butter and fill one side with mixture
4- Close pie iron and cook, turning frequently

HASHBROWNS

Ingredients:
Grated potatoes
Chopped onion
Butter

Directions:
1- Squeeze excess moisture from the potatoes
2- Combine the potatoes and onion
3- Grease pie iron with butter
4- Fill one half of pie iron with potato mixture
5- Close pie iron and cook, turning frequently

GROG CAKES

Ingredients:
1/2 cup dry milk
2 cups oatmeal (not instant)
1/4 tsp. cinnamon
1/4 tsp. nutmeg
2 tbsp. brown sugar
1 tsp. baking powder
1 egg (optional)
2 tbsp. oil
1 1/4 cups water
Butter

Directions:
1- Combine all dry ingredients in a plastic baggie (usually before trip)
2- Beat egg, oil, and dry ingredients together; let stand for 10 minutes
3- Grease pie iron with butter
4- Pour mixture into one half of the pie iron, then close and cook until lightly browned
5- Serve with honey, butter, jam or syrup

CHEESY TOTS

Ingredients:
Thawed tater tots
Minced onion
Minced green pepper
Garlic salt, salt, and pepper
Shredded cheddar cheese
Melted butter

Directions:
1- Add melted butter and make one layer of tater tots in one half of the pie iron
2- Add garlic salt, salt and pepper to taste
3- Add minced onion and green pepper
4- Close pie iron and cook 4-5 minutes per side
5- Open pie iron and add shredded cheese
6- Close pie iron and cook further until cheese is melted; do not turn pie iron over

PIE IRON CINNAMON STICKS

Ingredients:
Bread
8 oz. cream cheese
1 egg yolk
1 and 1/4 cup sugar, divided
2 tsp. cinnamon
1/2 cup butter, melted
1/4 tsp. vanilla

Directions:
1- Combine cream cheese, egg yolk, vanilla, and 1/4 cup sugar
2- Mix remaining sugar and cinnamon in separate flat dish
3- Remove crust from bread, then flatten
4- Spread cream cheese mixture on flattened bread
5- Roll bread up diagonally from point to point
6- Dip rolled up stick in melted butter, then roll in sugar and cinnamon mix
7- Add to pie iron (up to 3 can fit in a square one)
8- Cook over fire until golden brown and sugar is caramelized, turning at least once

Alternatives:
* Use pie filling as a fruit dip

SIMPLE CINNAMON ROLL TOAST

Ingredients:
Bread
3 tsp. cinnamon
3 tbsp. butter, softened
1/2 cup powdered sugar
Milk

Directions:
1- Mix butter and cinnamon
2- Mix milk and powdered sugar; add enough milk to allow for drizzling over toast
3- Spread butter mixture on both sides of one slice of bread
4- Cook bread slice until golden brown; drizzle with icing

POTATO, BACON & EGG BREAKFAST

Ingredients:
Mashed potatoes (leftover or instant)
Onions, minced (optional)
Eggs
Cheddar cheese, shredded
Bacon, cooked and crumbled
Salt and pepper
Butter, melted/softened

Directions:
1- Prepare mashed potatoes, adding onion if desired
2- Add butter to one half of pie iron, then add mashed potatoes
3- Make a divot in the potatoes and add cheese
4- Add egg to depression, then add bacon and salt & pepper to taste
5- Add butter to other half of pie iron
6- Cook on potato side first, then flip to finish cooking

EGG IN THE NEST

Ingredients:
Grated potatoes
Chopped onion
Hot sauce (optional)
Egg
Butter, melted/softened

Directions:
1- Squeeze excess moisture from the potatoes
2- Combine the potatoes and onion
3- Add butter, potatoes, and a dash of hot sauce, then cook over the fire for 3 minutes per side or until slightly brown
4- Open pie iron and make a small depression in the middle
5- Add egg to depression, then cook for additional 2-3 minutes, turning if desired

PACKED PANCAKE BREAKFAST

Ingredients:
Pancakes, precooked
Bacon, cooked and crumbled
Kielbasa, thinly sliced
Egg
Maple syrup
Butter

Directions:
1- Add butter and pancake to pie iron
2- Add egg, bacon, kielbasa, and a little maple syrup
3- Add another pancake and butter
4- Cook until egg is completely cooked, 2-3 minutes per side; serve with maple syrup

LUNCH/DINNER RECIPES

TUNA MELTS

Ingredients:
1 can tuna
Bread
Chopped pickle
Mayonnaise
Dijon mustard
Tomato, sliced
Sliced cheese
Butter

Directions:
1- Mix tuna, pickle, mayo, and mustard
2- Put a dab of butter into one side of the pie iron, then add a slice of bread
3- Add tuna mixture, a slice of cheese, and a slice of tomato
4- Add a second slice of bread and more butter
5- Close pie iron and cook until golden brown

SALMON JAFFE

Ingredients:
Bread
Thinly sliced fresh or smoked salmon
Thinly sliced onion
Brie or Camembert cheese, sliced
Butter

Directions:
1- Add butter and a slice of bread to one side of the pie iron
2- Add salmon, onion, and cheese
3- Add a second slice of bread and butter, then close pie iron
4- Cook until golden brown

SALMON OR TUNA CRISTO

Ingredients:
Bread
1 can salmon or tuna
Mayonnaise
Finely chopped onion
Egg
1 tbsp. milk
Butter

Directions:
1- Mix salmon/tuna, mayonnaise and onion
2- In a separate container, mix the egg and milk
3- Add butter to one half of pie iron
4- Dip a bread slice into egg and milk mixture, then put in pie iron
5- Add salmon/tuna mixture
6- Dip other bread slice into egg and milk mixture and put on top
7- Close pie iron and cook until golden brown

CRAB PIE

Ingredients:
Bread
Canned crab or crab flavored Pollock flakes
Cream cheese, Brie or Camembert cheese slices
Diced onion
Butter

Directions:
1- Add butter and a slice of bread to one side of the pie iron
2- Add crab, onion, and cheese
3- Add a second slice of bread and butter, then close pie iron
4- Cook until golden brown

CHICKEN BBQ PIE

Ingredients:
Bread (Italian bread works well)
Sliced chicken breast (or deli sliced chicken)
Sliced Canadian bacon
Shredded Monterrey jack or mozzarella cheese
Your favorite BBQ sauce
Butter

Directions:
1- Add butter and a slice of bread to one side of the pie iron
2- Add chicken, bacon, cheese and BBQ sauce
3- Add a second slice of bread and butter, then close pie iron
4- Cook until golden brown

CHICKEN QUESEDILLAS

Ingredients:
Flour tortillas
Precooked, diced chicken
Canned green chilies (optional)
Diced onions and peppers
Grated mozzarella and cheddar cheese
Salsa
Butter

Directions:
1- Add butter and tortilla shell to one half of pie iron
2- Add chicken, chilies, onions, peppers and cheese
3- Add another tortilla shell and butter, then close pie iron
4- Cook until golden brown, then serve with salsa

Alternatives:
* Use beef or shrimp instead of chicken

GRILLED TURKEY

Ingredients:
Bread
Deli turkey breast slices
Swiss cheese slices
Thousand island dressing
Butter

Directions:
1- Add butter and a slice of bread to one side of the pie iron
2- Spread salad dressing on the unbuttered side of the bread slice
3- Add turkey slices and cheese
4- Add second bread slice and butter
5- Close pie iron and cook until golden brown

CHICKEN PARMESAN

Ingredients:
Bread
Sliced chicken breast (or deli sliced chicken)
Pizza sauce
Parmesan cheese
Mozzarella cheese
Butter

Directions:
1- Add butter and a slice of bread to one side of the pie iron
2- Spread pizza sauce on the unbuttered side of the bread slice
3- Add sliced chicken and sprinkle with Parmesan and mozzarella cheeses
4- Add second bread slice and butter
5- Close pie iron and cook until golden brown

Alternatives:
* Use a cooked veal cutlet instead of chicken

CHICKEN CORDON BLEU

Ingredients:
Bread
Sliced chicken breast (or deli sliced chicken)
Sliced ham
Swiss cheese slices
Sour cream
Can mushroom soup
White wine
Butter

Directions:
1- Combine 1 tablespoon each of sour cream and mushroom soup, plus 1 teaspoon of white wine
2- Add butter and a slice of bread to one side of the pie iron
3- Add 2 slices of chicken, 1 slice of ham, 1 slice of Swiss cheese, and the sour cream/mushroom soup mixture
4- Add second bread slice and butter
5- Close pie iron and cook until golden brown

GREEK PIE

Ingredients:
Bread
Diced chicken, pre-cooked
Feta cheese, crumbled
Mozzarella cheese, shredded
Olives
Artichokes
Butter

Directions:
1- Add butter and a slice of bread to one side of the pie iron
2- Add chicken, cheeses, olives and artichokes
3- Add second bread slice and butter
4- Close pie iron and cook until golden brown

SAMOSA PIE

Ingredients:
Bread
Diced chicken, pre-cooked
Canned peas and carrots
Baked potato, diced
Curry powder
Butter

Directions:
1- Add butter and a slice of bread to one side of the pie iron
2- Add chicken, vegetables and potatoe
3- Sprinkle curry powder to taste
4- Add second bread slice and butter
5- Close pie iron and cook until golden brown

GRILLED HAM AND CHEESE

Ingredients:
Bread
Sliced deli ham
Your favorite cheese
Dijon mustard
Butter

Directions:
1- Add butter and a slice of bread to one side of the pie iron
2- Spread mustard on unbuttered side of bread
3- Add ham and cheese
4- Add second bread slice and butter
5- Close pie iron and cook until golden brown

BLT SPECIAL

Ingredients:
Bread
Pre-cooked bacon slices
Tomato slices
Cheddar cheese slices
Shredded lettuce (optional)
Mayonnaise
Butter

Directions:
1- Add butter and a slice of bread to one side of the pie iron
2- Spread mayonnaise on unbuttered side of bread
3- Add bacon, tomato, cheese and lettuce
4- Add second bread slice and butter
5- Close pie iron and cook until golden brown

CUBAN SANDWICH

Ingredients:
Rye bread
Thinly sliced ham
Thinly sliced pork
Swiss cheese
Flat pickles
Mustard
Butter

Directions:
1- Add butter and a slice of bread to one side of the pie iron
2- Spread mustard on unbuttered side of bread
3- Add the ham, pork, pickles, and cheese
4- Add second bread slice and butter
5- Close pie iron and cook until golden brown

REUBEN SANDWICH

Ingredients:
Rye or pumpernickel bread
Cooked corned beef
Sauerkraut
Swiss cheese, sliced
Russian dressing
Butter

Directions:
1- Add butter and a slice of bread to one side of the pie iron
2- Add the corned beef, sauerkraut, dressing and cheese
3- Add second bread slice and butter
4- Close pie iron and cook until golden brown

Alternatives:
* Use coleslaw for a sweeter variety

GRILLED ROAST BEEF SANDWICH

Ingredients:
Rye bread
1 tbsp mayonnaise
1/2 tbsp Dijon mustard
Swiss cheese, sliced
Thinly sliced roast beef
Salsa or picante sauce (optional)
Butter

Directions:
1- Combine mayonnaise and mustard
2- Add butter and a slice of bread to one side of the pie iron
3- Spread mustard on unbuttered side of bread
4- Add the roast beef and cheese; add salsa/picante if desired
5- Add second bread slice and butter
6- Close pie iron and cook until golden brown

BURRITO

Ingredients:
Prepared taco meat
Salsa
Cheddar cheese
Grilled onions and peppers
Sour cream
Shredded lettuce
Flour tortillas
Butter

Directions:
1- Add butter and a tortilla to one side of the pie iron
2- Add taco meat, cheese, and onions and peppers
3- Add second tortilla and butter
4- Close pie iron and cook until golden brown; serve with lettuce, sour cream and salsa

Alternatives:
* For a meatless variety, use re-fried beans instead of taco meat

PHILLY CHEESESTEAK

Ingredients:
Bread (Italian is best)
Thinly sliced steak
Finely chopped onion, pepper and mushroom
Sliced cheese, your favorite variety
Pizza or BBQ sauce (optional)
Butter

Directions:
1- Add butter and a slice of bread to one side of the pie iron
2- Add meat, onion, pepper, mushroom, cheese, and sauce
3- Add second bread slice and butter
4- Close pie iron and cook until golden brown

BACON CHEESEBURGER

Ingredients:
Bread
1/4 cup pre-cooked hamburger, crumbled
Bacon, pre-cooked
Cheese slices, your favorite
Butter

Directions:
1- Add butter and a slice of bread to one side of the pie iron
2- Add hamburger, bacon, and cheese
3- Add second bread slice and butter
4- Close pie iron and cook until golden brown

BEEF STEW PIE

Ingredients:
Pie pastry
Canned beef stew
Butter

Directions:
1- Add butter and put half of the pie pastry on one side of the pie iron
2- Add beef stew
3- Fold over rest of pie pastry and add butter
4- Close pie iron and cook until golden brown

PASTIES

Ingredients:
Pie pastry
Cooked cubed steak
Cooked potato cubes/slices
Onions
Italian seasoning
Butter

Directions:
1- Add butter and put half of the pie pastry on one side of the pie iron
2- Add steak, potatoes, onion, a bad of butter, and Italian seasonings
3- Fold over rest of pie pastry and add butter
4- Close pie iron and cook until golden brown

SLOPPY JOES

Ingredients:
Bread
Sloppy-joe mix (homemade or bought)
Butter

Directions:
1- Add butter and a slice of bread
2- Add sloppy joe mix
3- Add another slice of bread and add butter
4- Close pie iron and cook until golden brown

Alternatives:
* Add shredded cheddar cheese with the sloppy joe mix
* Add chopped onion with the mix

MEATLOAF SANDWICH

Ingredients:
Bread
Meatloaf, sliced
Sliced cheese, your favorite
Tomato, sliced
Onion, sliced
Butter

Directions:
1- Add butter and a slice of bread
2- Add meatloaf, onion, tomato, and cheese
3- Add another slice of bread and add butter
4- Close pie iron and cook until golden brown

Alternatives:
* Add ketchup or BBQ sauce

GRILLED CHEESE

Ingredients:
Bread
Sliced cheese, your favorite
Onion (optional)
Butter

Directions:
1- Add butter and a slice of bread
2- Add cheese and onion
3- Add another slice of bread and add butter
4- Close pie iron and cook until golden brown

CALZONE

Ingredients:
Pillsbury pizza crust dough
Cooked spinach
Chopped onion
Sliced mushrooms
Minced garlic
White pasta sauce
Shredded mozzarella cheese
Pine nuts (optional)
Artichokes (optional)
Butter

Directions:
1- In 1/2 of the pie iron, saute onion, mushrooms and garlic in butter
2- In the other half of pie iron, put a piece of butter and pizza dough, then add sauted veggies
3- Add spinach, cheese, pine nuts and artichokes; drizzle pasta sauce over everything
4- Add another piece of pizza dough and butter
5- Close pie iron and cook until golden brown

PB & J

Ingredients:
Bread
Peanut butter
Your favorite jam/jelly
Butter

Directions:
1- Add butter and a slice of bread
2- Add peanut butter and jam/jelly
3- Add another slice of bread and add butter
4- Close pie iron and cook until golden brown

MAC & CHEESE POCKET

Ingredients:
Bread
Prepared macaroni and cheese
Butter

Directions:
1- Add butter and a slice of bread
2- Add macaroni and cheese
3- Add another slice of bread and add butter
4- Close pie iron and cook until golden brown

Alternatives:
* Add crumbled bacon

PEPPER POPPERS

Ingredients:
Refrigerated biscuits
Cream cheese
Bacon, cooked and crumbled
Jalepeno peppers, chopped
Butter

Directions:
1- Mix the cream cheese, bacon and Jalepeno peppers
2- Add butter and one of the biscuits
3- Add pepper mixture
4- Add another biscuit and add butter
5- Close pie iron and cook until golden brown, cooking slowly at first so the biscuits don't burn

BASIC PIZZA POCKETS

Ingredients:
Bread
Pizza sauce
Shredded cheese, your favorite
Butter

Directions:
1- Add butter and one slice of bread
2- Add pizza sauce and shredded cheese
3- Add another bread slice and add butter
4- Close pie iron and cook until golden brown

Alternatives:
* Add your favorite meat(s), like sausage, canadian bacon, pepperoni, or hamburger
* Make a veggie pizza with onions, pepper, and tomatoes
* Make specialty pizzas like hawaiian (ham and pineapple) or BBQ chicken (diced chicken, bacon and BBQ sauce instead of pizza sauce)

CHICKEN POT PIE

Ingredients:
Tube of crescent rolls
Cooked chicken breast strips
Can of mixed vegetables
1 tsp chicken bullion granules
Can of cream of chicken soup
Salt and pepper
Butter

Directions:
1- Mix chicken breast strips, cream of chicken soup, vegetables and chicken bullion; keep refrigerated
2- Add butter and one of the unrolled crescent pieces
3- Add chicken mixture
4- Add another piece of unrolled crescent roll
5- Close pie iron and cook until golden brown

SPAGHETTI SANDWICHES

Ingredients:
Bread (Italian bread works well)
Spaghetti noodles, cooked
Spaghetti sauce
Garlic powder or crushed garlic
Italian seasoning
Butter

Directions:
1- Add butter, garlic and Italian seasonings, then add a slice of bread to one side of the pie iron
2- Add spaghetti and sauce
3- Add a second slice of bread, then add butter, garlic and Italian seasonings
4- Close pie iron and cook until golden brown, turning often

Alternatives:
* Add cooked sausage along with the noodles and sauce
* Add Parmesan cheese

BOLOGNA & CHEESE SANDWICHES

Ingredients:
Bread
Bologna
Colby and Monterey jack cheeses, shredded
Onions, chopped
Mustard
Mayonnaise
Butter

Directions:
1- Add butter and a slice of bread to one side of the pie iron
2- Spread mayonnaise on both slices of bread
3- Add bologna, onion, mustard, and shredded cheeses
4- Add a second slice of bread and butter
5- Close pie iron and cook until golden brown

RAVIOLI WITH GARLIC TOAST

Ingredients:
Ravioli, any kind
Garlic Texas toast
Shredded cheese, your favorite kind
Spaghetti sauce
Butter

Directions:
1- Add butter and a slice of Texas toast
2- Add ravioli, sauce and cheese
3- Add another slice of Texas toast and butter
4- Close pie iron and cook until golden brown

BACON & PEANUT BUTTER

Ingredients:
Bread
Crunchy peanut butter
Bacon, cooked
Butter

Directions:
1- Add butter and a slice of bread to one side of the pie iron
2- Spread peanut butter on both slices of bread
3- Add bacon
4- Add a second slice of bread and butter
5- Close pie iron and cook until golden brown

BAKED BEANS SANDWICH

Ingredients:
Bread
Baked beans, any variety
Butter

Directions:
1- Add butter and a slice of bread to one side of the pie iron
2- Add baked beans
3- Add a second slice of bread and butter
4- Close pie iron and cook until golden brown

Alternatives:
* Add fried onion
* Add cooked bacon

CHICKEN & PINEAPPLE

Ingredients:
Bread
Cooked chicken, cubed
Shredded cheddar cheese
Onion, sliced
Mayonnaise
Pineapple, crushed and drained
Tomato, diced
Sweet chili sauce (optional)
Butter

Directions:
1- Add butter and a slice of bread to one side of the pie iron
2- Spread mayonnaise on both slices of bread
3- Add chicken, onion, pineapple, tomato, and sweet chili sauce
4- Add a second slice of bread and butter
5- Close pie iron and cook until golden brown

HOT BBQ BEEF SANDWICH

Ingredients:
Bread
Roast beef, thinly sliced
BBQ sauce
Prepared mashed potatoes
Butter

Directions:
1- Cut roast beef into strips and stir in BBQ sauce
2- Add butter and a slice of bread to one side of the pie iron
3- Add BBQ roast beef and mashed potatoes
4- Add a second slice of bread and butter
5- Close pie iron and cook until golden brown

VEGETARIAN QUESADILLA

Ingredients:
Flour tortillas
Refried beans
Shredded cheddar cheese
Salsa
Butter

Directions:
1- Add butter and a tortilla to one side of the pie iron
2- Add refried beans and shredded cheese
3- Add second tortilla and butter
4- Close pie iron and cook until golden brown; serve with salsa

EASY VEGAN HOBO PIE

Ingredients:
Flour tortillas
Black beans
Kernel corn
Salsa
Butter

Directions:
1- Add butter and a tortilla to one side of the pie iron
2- Add black beans, kernel corn, and salsa
3- Add second tortilla and butter
4- Close pie iron and cook until golden brown; serve with salsa

Alternatives:
* Substitute other fillings as desired: rice, potatoes, onions, peppers

DESSERT RECIPES

CHOCOLATE CARAMEL PIE

Ingredients:
Tube of crescent rolls
Caramel pieces
Chocolate chips
Mini marshmallows
Butter

Directions:
1- Add butter and a square of crescent rolls
2- Add caramels, chocolate chips and mini marshmallows
3- Add another square of crescent rolls and add butter
4- Close pie iron and cook until golden brown

Alternatives:
* Substitute peanut butter instead of caramel

CINNAMON BUN PIE

Ingredients:
Tube of crescent rolls
Cinnamon and sugar mixture
Chocolate chips
Mini marshmallows
Raisins (optional)
Chopped walnuts (optional)
Butter

Directions:
1- Add butter and a square of crescent rolls
2- Add cinnamon and sugar mixture, chocolate chips, mini marshmallows, raisins and walnuts
3- Add another square of crescent rolls and add butter
4- Close pie iron and cook until golden brown

BASIC FRUIT TURNOVER

Ingredients:
Bread
Can of favorite pie filling
Confectioners sugar
Butter

Directions:
1- Add butter and a slice of bread
2- Add fruit pie filling
3- Add another slice of bread and butter
4- Close pie iron and cook until golden brown; dust with confectioner sugar

Alternatives:
* Use cinnamon swirl bread
* Use angel food cake instead of bread

APPLE STRUDEL

Ingredients:
Tube of crescent rolls
Cinnamon and sugar mixture
Can of apple pie filling
Raisins (optional)
Butter

Directions:
1- mix apple pie filling, cinnamon and sugar mixture, and raisins
2- Add butter and a square of crescent rolls
3- Add apple pie filling mixture
4- Add another square of crescent rolls and add butter
5- Close pie iron and cook until golden brown

CHERRY CHEESECAKE DESSERT

Ingredients:
Bread
Can cherry pie filling
Mini marshmallows
Cream cheese
Butter

Directions:
1- Add butter and a slice of bread
2- Spread softened cream cheese on both slices of bread
3- Add cherry pie filling and mini marshmallows
4- Add another slice of bread and butter
5- Close pie iron and cook until golden brown

LEMON MERINGUE PIE

Ingredients:
Bread
Can lemon pie filling
Mini marshmallows
Butter

Directions:
1- Add butter and a slice of bread
2- Add lemon pie filling and mini marshmallows
3- Add another slice of bread and butter
4- Close pie iron and cook until golden brown

PEANUT BUTTER CUP MELT

Ingredients:
Bread
Peanut butter
Chocolate chips
Butter

Directions:
1- Add butter and a slice of bread
2- Add peanut butter and chocolate chips
3- Add another slice of bread and butter
4- Close pie iron and cook until golden brown

SUNNY PEACH SANDWICH

Ingredients:
Bread
1 canned peach half
Mini marshmallows
Butter

Directions:
1- Add butter and a slice of bread
2- Add mini marshmallows to the hollow of the peach, then put peach on bread
3- Add another slice of bread and butter
4- Close pie iron and cook until golden brown

BANANA CREAM PIE

Ingredients:
Bread
Sliced banana
Mini marshmallows
Butter

Directions:
1- Add butter and a slice of bread
2- Add sliced banana and mini marshmallows
3- Add another slice of bread and butter
4- Close pie iron and cook until golden brown

Alternatives:
* Add chocolate chips

FLUFFERNUTTER PIE

Ingredients:
Bread
Marshmallow fluff
Peanut butter or Nutella
Butter

Directions:
1- Add butter and a slice of bread
2- Add peanut butter or Nutella and marshmallow fluff
3- Add another slice of bread and butter
4- Close pie iron and cook until golden brown

CINNAMON & SUGAR PIE

Ingredients:
Tube of crescent rolls
Cinnamon and sugar mixture
Butter

Directions:
1- Add butter and a square of crescent rolls
2- Add cinnamon and sugar mixture
3- Add another square of crescent rolls and add butter
4- Close pie iron and cook until golden brown

Alternatives:
* Add raisins with the cinnamon and sugar

Darren Kirby

PEANUT BUTTER & MARSHMALLOWS

Ingredients:
Bread
Peanut butter
Marshmallows
Butter

Directions:
1- Add butter and a slice of bread
2- Add peanut butter and marshmallows
3- Add another slice of bread and add butter
4- Close pie iron and cook until golden brown

Alternatives:
* Add bananas with the marshmallows and peanut butter

CREAM CHEESE & FRESH BERRIES

Ingredients:
Bread
Cream cheese
Fresh berries, sliced, any kind
Butter

Directions:
1- Add butter and a slice of bread
2- Spread cream cheese on both slices of bread
3- Add sliced berries
4- Add the other slice of bread and add butter
5- Close pie iron and cook until golden brown

Alternatives:
* Use your favorite jam instead of berries

NUTTY-CREAMY-FRUITY GOODNESS

Ingredients:
Bread
Cream cheese
Fresh strawberries, sliced
Nutella
Butter

Directions:
1- Add butter and a slice of bread
2- Spread cream cheese on both slices of bread
3- Add sliced berries and Nutella
4- Add the other slice of bread and add butter
5- Close pie iron and cook until golden brown

CHOCOLATE CARAMEL NUT PIES

Ingredients:
Bread
Caramel candies
Chocolate chips
Chopped pecans
Butter

Directions:
1- Add butter and a slice of bread
2- Add caramels, chocolate chips, and pecans
3- Add another slice of bread and add butter
4- Close pie iron and cook until golden brown

Alternatives:
* Try walnuts, peanuts, or cashews instead of pecans

BANANA & NUTELLA

Ingredients:
Bread
Banana, sliced
Nutella
Butter

Directions:
1- Add butter and a slice of bread
2- Spread Nutella on both slices of bread
3- Add sliced banana
4- Add the other slice of bread and butter
5- Close pie iron and cook until golden brown

APPLE & BROWN SUGAR

Ingredients:
Raisin bread
Granny smith apple, thinly sliced
Lemon juice
Brown sugar
Cinnamon
Butter

Directions:
1- Add butter and a slice of raisin bread
2- Add apple, brown sugar, cinnamon (to taste), and sprinkle with lemon juice
3- Add the other slice of bread and butter
4- Close pie iron and cook until golden brown

PEANUT BUTTER & APPLES

Ingredients:
Bread
Peanut butter
Apples, thinly sliced
Butter

Directions:
1- Add butter and a slice of bread
2- Spread peanut butter on both slices
3- Add apples
4- Add another slice of bread and butter
5- Close pie iron and cook until golden brown

Alternatives:
* Use raisin bread instead of regular bread

PUMPKIN PIE

Ingredients:
Bread
Pumpkin pie filling
Mini marshmallows
Cinnamon
Butter

Directions:
1- Add butter and a slice of bread
2- Add pumpkin pie filling, mini marshmallows, and cinnamon
3- Add another slice of bread and butter
4- Close pie iron and cook until golden brown

CINNAMON BALLS

Ingredients:
Canned biscuits
Cinnamon and sugar, mixed
Melted butter

Directions:
1- Open biscuits and roll into balls
2- Dip the biscuit balls into the melted butter, then roll in the cinnamon and sugar mix
3- Put in pie iron and cook until golden brown

BERRIES & CHOCOLATE

Ingredients:
Bread
Cherry or raspberry pie filling
Chocolate chips
Butter

Directions:
1- Add butter and a slice of bread
2- Add pie filling and chocolate chips
3- Add another slice of bread and butter
4- Close pie iron and cook until golden brown

CARAMEL APPLE PIE

Ingredients:
Bread
Apple, thinly sliced
Caramel ice cream topping
Butter

Directions:
1- Add butter and a slice of bread
2- Add apples and top with caramel sauce
3- Add another slice of bread and butter
4- Close pie iron and cook until golden brown

PINEAPPLE DELIGHT

Ingredients:
Bread
Crushed pineapple, well-drained
Mini marshmallows
Butter

Directions:
1- Add butter and a slice of bread
2- Add crushed pineapple and mini marshmallows
3- Add another slice of bread and butter
4- Close pie iron and cook until golden brown

Alternatives:
* Add coconut flakes

CHOCOLATE CHEESECAKE

Ingredients:
Bread
2 eggs
3 tbsp milk
2 tsp brown sugar
1 tsp vanilla
2/3 cup graham cracker crumbs
1/2 cup cream cheese, softened
1/2 cup chocolate hazelnut spread
Butter

Directions:
1- In small bowl, whisk together eggs, milk, sugar, and vanilla
2- Pour graham crumbs into separate shallow dish
3- In medium bowl, stir together cream cheese and chocolate hazelnut spread until no lumps remain
4- Spread 1/4 cup of cream cheese mixture onto 1 slice bread; top with another slice of bread
5- Dip sandwich into egg mixture just long enough to soak bread on each side, then dredge in graham crumbs
6- Place sandwich in greased pie iron and bake on hot coals, turning every 2 minutes, until bread is toasted and crispy and graham crumbs are browned, about 6 to 8 minutes

CAMPFIRE CHOCOLATE MONKEY BREAD

Ingredients:
Refrigerated biscuits
1/2 cup brown sugar
1 package chocolate cook and serve pudding (not instant mix)
1/4 cup sugar
1/2 cup butter
Additional butter

Directions:
1- Place the brown sugar, pudding mix, and sugar into a large Ziploc bag
2- Cut up the biscuits into quarters; drop into the Ziploc bag and completely cover
3- Melt the butter and pour over the biscuits; reseal Ziploc bag and shake
4- Add a little of the extra melted butter to the pie iron and add 1-2 biscuits
5- Close pie iron and cook for 10-12 minutes, turning frequently

CHOCOLATE OVERLOAD

Ingredients:
Bread
Nutella
Chocolate bar with nuts
Butter

Directions:
1- Add butter and a slice of bread
2- Spread Nutella on both slices, then add pieces of broken chocolate bar with nuts
3- Add the other slice of bread and butter
4- Close pie iron and cook until golden brown

ADDITIONAL FOOD RECIPES

FRIED POTATOES

Ingredients:
Sliced potatoes
Sliced onion (optional)
Salt and pepper (optional)
Butter

Directions:
1- Add sliced potatoes, onions, and butter to one half of the pie iron
2- Add salt and pepper to taste
3- Close pie iron and cook until done

GRILLED MUSHROOMS

Ingredients:
Sliced mushrooms
Parsley
White wine/beer
Salt and pepper (optional)
Butter

Directions:
1- Add sliced mushrooms, parsley, splash of white wine, and butter to one half of the pie iron
2- Add salt and pepper to taste
3- Close pie iron and cook until done

GRILLED ONIONS

Ingredients:
Sliced onions
Parsley
White wine/beer
Salt and pepper (optional)
Butter

Directions:
1- Add sliced onions, parsley, splash of white wine, and butter to one half of the pie iron
2- Add salt and pepper to taste
3- Close pie iron and cook until done

BISCUITS

Ingredients:
Can buttermilk biscuits
Melted butter

Directions:
1- Open biscuit can and separate
2- Cut biscuits in half and roll into balls
3- Roll in melted butter and put into pie iron
4- Close pie iron and cook until done

Alternatives:
* Add cinnamon and sugar after rolling ball in melted butter
* Add garlic salt after rolling ball in melted butter

CORNBREAD

Ingredients:
Box cornbread mix
Melted butter

Directions:
1- Prepare cornbread according to directions
2- Add melted butter to both halves of pie iron
3- Pour cornbread mixture into one half of the pie iron
4- Close pie iron and cook about a minute, then turn over and cook another minute or until done

Alternatives:
* Add shredded cheddar cheese and chopped canned chilies to taste

BRIE IN PASTRY

Ingredients:
Pie pastry
Small pieces of Brie
Sun-dried tomatoes
Melted butter

Directions:
1- Add butter pie pastry to one half of pie iron
2- Add brie and tomatoes
3- Add pie pastry and butter
4- Close pie iron and cook until golden brown
5- Serve with crackers and/or apple slices and white wine

GARLIC CHEESE BALLS

Ingredients:
Can buttermilk biscuits
Garlic
Parmesan Cheese
Melted butter

Directions:
1- Open biscuit can and separate
2- Cut biscuits in half and roll into balls
3- Roll in melted butter, then add cheese and garlic and put into pie iron
4- Close pie iron and cook until done

GRILLED STEAK

Ingredients:
Sirloin or cube steak, cut into strips
Olive oil
Mushrooms
Onions
Green peppers
Seasonings

Directions:
1- Add strips of steak to one half of the pie iron and add your favorite seasoning
2- Add cut peppers, onions, and mushrooms
3- Add a splash of olive oil
4- Close pie iron and cook until done

PORTABELLA MELTS

Ingredients:
Large portabella mushroom caps
Mozzarella cheese, sliced
Thousand island dressing
Butter

Directions:
1- Turn over mushroom cap and scrape out the gills with a spoon
2- Butter both half of the pie iron and place the mushroom cap in the pie iron
3- Sear mushroom cap over the fire for a few minutes on each side
4- Open the pie iron and add dressing into the mushroom cap, then add a slice of cheese
5- Close the pie iron and cook until the cheese is melted; do not turn pie iron over

HONEY GLAZED CARROTS

Ingredients:
Frozen sliced carrots
1 and 1/2 tbsp honey
1 tsp butter
1 tsp parsley flakes
1 tsp mustard (optional)

Directions:
1- Combine all ingredients and spoon into one half of the pie iron
2- Close the pie iron and cook until heated through, turning and shaking frequently

PUDGIE FRIED RICE

Ingredients:
2 cups white rice
2 tbsp soy sauce
1 tsp minced garlic
1-2 beaten eggs
1 cup of drained fillings of your choice: various cooked meats, peas, beans or other finely chopped veggies

Directions:
1- Combine all ingredients and mix thoroughly
2- Add mixture to both halves of the pie iron
3- Close the pie iron and cook 3-5 minutes or until heated through

Pie Iron Recipes

HELPFUL HINTS WHEN USING YOUR PIE IRON

* Use tin foil in your pie irons. Not only does this help prevent cross contamination (i.e., preventing your desert from tasting like your meal), but it also aids in cleaning up.
* Keep a pot holder close by as the latch/clasp will be hot and difficult to open
* Having a good bed of hot coals will help your pies to cook faster and more evenly
* Use your imagination for what to put into a pie, and have fun!

Pie Iron Recipes

ALUMINUM VS CAST IRON

When you go out looking for your first (or next) pie iron, you will quickly notice that there are two different types of them: the shiny aluminum type, and the dark cast iron type. One is the traditional, and one is the contemporary. Let's look at a few attributes of each.

Weight. As you might guess, the aluminum version is the lighter of the two. This makes them easier to carry around and easier to handle while cooking. Plus, they are easier to manipulate for the youngsters in your life. The case iron ones are definitely heavier, no bones about it.

Clean up. Cast iron cleans up quickly and easily, and can be scrubbed with an abrasive scrubber without damaging them. As the cast iron is "seasoned" by regular use, it becomes easier to clean. It is recommended that you protect them afterward with a light coating of grease to help prevent oxidation. The aluminum version typically is coated with Teflon on the interior. This allows for food to easily slip out after cooking, making cleaning a snap. However, this requires you to be more gentle with your washing, i.e., no abrasive scrubbers. Also, there is a real risk that the Teflon may start to flake off, whether from use, careless handling or accidental damage.

Cost. The aluminum version typically costs a few dollars less than the cast iron counterpart.

Durability. Many might argue this, but I feel the cast iron version can take a beating and still make great pudgie pies. Because the aluminum can dent, the Teflon coating can come off, and they generally need to be treated more gently, cast iron is the more durable of the two. Also, because aluminum has a lower melting point than cast iron, you will often hear of people getting their aluminum pie irons too hot (by resting them on hot coals, etc.) and then they warp, causing them to not work as well or at all.

Cooking. Because of the metal used, aluminum pie irons cook faster because they transfer heat faster. This can lead to pies that are burned on the outside, yet uncooked/undercooked on the inside. You can burn pies in the cast iron as well, but it's much more forgiving in my experience.

So, where does that leave us? Well, in the end, I feel that the cast iron version is the better choice. You don't have to treat them with "kid gloves" like you do with the aluminum kind, you don't have to worry about your pie iron warping from the intense heat, and they cook more even than the aluminum kind. Sure, you'll pay a few dollars more for the cast iron, but they make up for that in spades by having a much longer life of providing tasty meals. We have had our cast iron ones for many years, and after having tried the aluminum kind, we got rid of them because they just were inferior to the cast iron.

PIE IRON CARRY CASE

Pie irons are great for cooking, but don't always fit neatly into your camping gear. Or, they become more of a pain to bring with when going out to a picnic, etc. Here's a fun way to carry your pie irons while also making use of worn-out jeans.

Jean legs make the perfect carrying case. Once you cut off the leg, turn it inside out and sew up one end, leaving the other end open. If you like, while it's still inside out, you can sew on a cloth strap for easier carrying. You can also apply a hook-and-loop fastener to the top edge of the open end so that you can close up the case. Easy instructions are readily available on Pinterest and other social media platforms.

Another idea that a friend of mine did was to build a box out of scrap wood. Build a frame that is slightly longer than your pie irons. 1x4 lumber is great for this purpose. Use plywood for the top and bottom of the box. Add a couple of hinges for the lid, and add a latch of some kind to keep the lid on. Last, add a handle to the side where the latch is for easy carrying.

Either one of these simple projects can be completed in an hour or so, and will make transporting your pie irons much easier, as well as storing them. Have fun decorating them as well!

Pie Iron Recipes

SEASONING YOUR CAST IRON PIE IRON

All new cast iron cookware are coated with paraffin wax at the factory to prevent rust. It's important to clean or cook off the wax and then season your new pie iron before you use it. Proper seasoning will create a beautiful, non-stick finish on your cast iron for years of worry-free use.

Ingredients:
Solid vegetable shortening
Scrub brush
Wash bins
Dish soap
Paper towels
Charcoal grill or campfire

Directions:
1- Clean new pie irons by separating at the hinges and then heating over a charcoal grill or campfire for about 10 minutes, flipping halfway through, to remove the wax. Let cool for a few minutes. While still warm, scour with a bristle scrub brush and hot soapy water. Dry completely and follow the directions below to season immediately
2- Season pie irons by coating the entire surface of the cast iron, inside and out, with vegetable shortening. Heat, bowl side up, over

a charcoal grill or campfire for about 15 minutes, flipping halfway through. Let cool. Recoat with shortening and heat again. Repeat this process two more times. Let cool. Recoat with shortening to prevent rust during storage

3- After each use, wipe your pie iron clean with a paper towel or hot water and a soft brush or sponge. (do not use soap!) Dry completely and apply a light coat of oil or shortening to prevent rust during storage

4- Cast iron will become darker and well seasoned after repeated use

ABOUT THE AUTHOR

Darren holds down a normal job by day, and lets his weird side show at night in his writings. He has held a number of different jobs: Financial Analyst, Frozen Food Manager, Pizza Merchandiser, Product Manager, Grocery Bagger, Computer Training Salesperson, Coffee Shop Owner. All along the way, his love of the written word has remained and festered in the far reaches of his mind. Today, he is a budding novelist and short story writer. "Pie Iron Recipes" is his first recipe book, "Sometimes They Scream" is his first short story collection, and "Coordinates For Murder" is his first novel. He lives in the north woods of Wisconsin with his beloved wife and two mischievous felines.

CONNECT WITH THE AUTHOR

I would love to hear from you! Let me know what you think of this book or any of my other short stories or novels. And thanks for choosing to read my works!

Email:
dlk.writer@gmail.com

Website:
www.darrenkirby.com

Facebook:
www.facebook.com/darrenleekirby

LinkedIn:
www.linkedin.com/in/darrenkirby

Twitter:
www.twitter.com/darrenleekirby